A LOOK AROUND Coral Reefs

by Tracey E. Dils

Published by Willowisp Press
801 94th Avenue North, St. Petersburg, Florida 33702

Copyright © 1995 by Willowisp Press,
a division of PAGES, Inc.

Printed in the United States of America

2 4 6 8 10 9 7 5 3 1

ISBN 0-87406-728-6

To Claudia,
because you understand the ways of the wrasse fish.

And to Emily and Phillip:
May you become watchers of the world and keepers of the reef.

Acknowledgments

Thanks to Mrs. Mayr's and Mrs. McAtee's first-grade classes at Barrington School
for taking me on the field trip that inspired this book.
And to Claudia Y. W. Herrold for the research assistance she provided.

Photo Credits
All photographs from Tom Stack & Associates

Photographers as listed: Front cover by Brian Parker, Randy Morse (hermit crab), Dave B. Fleetham (white-tip reef shark and seahorse). Photographs on p. 4-5 by Manfred Gottschalk, Tammy Peluso (inset), Mike Bacon (inset); p. 6-7 by Dave B. Fleetham, Brian Parker (inset), Denise Tackett (inset); p. 8 by Randy Morse; p. 9 by Brian Parker; p. 10 by Tammy Peluso, p. 11 by Denise Tackett; p. 12 by Larry Lipsky; p. 13 by Dave B. Fleetham; p. 14 by Brian Parker; p. 15 by Jack Reid, Dave B. Fleetham (inset); p. 16 by Dave B. Fleetham; p. 17 by Tom Stack; p. 18 by Larry Lipsky; p. 19 by Brian Parker, Dave B. Fleetham (inset); p. 20 by Dave B. Fleetham; p. 21 by Jack Reid; p. 22 by Dave B. Fleetham; p. 23 Cindy Garoutte/PDS; p. 24-25 Mike Severns, Dave B. Fleetham (inset); p. 26-27 by M. Timothy O'Keefe, Manfred Gottschalk (inset); p. 28-29 Dave B. Fleetham, D. Holden Bailey (inset). Back cover photograph by Mike Bacon.

Table of Contents

A Strange Underwater World

Just below the ocean, there is a strange underwater world. Red, wavy fans sway to and fro. Blue stony fingers reach upward. Strange blue and red flowers wave their petals. Tiny sea horses glide through the water. Fish dart back and forth. Giant stars hug the ocean's bottom.

Welcome to the mysterious and beautiful coral reef.

Coral reefs are found only in shallow water near the *equator*. That's an imaginary line that divides the earth into two halves. It is also the warmest part of the earth.

Coral reefs are a kind of underwater neighborhood, or *habitat*. Thousands of plants and animals live there. The coral reef may be home to more different kinds of plants and animals than anywhere else on earth.

4

What Is Coral?

Coral found on a beach or in a store may look like a kind of stone. But under water, coral can look like giant fans or pieces of lettuce. Some types of coral even look like brains!

Coral is made up of many tiny animals called **polyps.** Most polyps are about the size of a pea. Polyps build the coral reefs. When a polyp attaches itself to a rock, it builds a stony house around its body. The house, or skeleton, is the shape of a cup. It is made of a stone called *limestone.*

Millions of polyps build their houses together to form a coral reef. When old polyps die, new ones build their houses on top of them. Over thousands of years, a coral reef can grow to be a thousand miles long.

The outside of the reef is the only place where there are live coral polyps. At night, these polyps use long arms, called *tentacles,* to sting tiny animals. Then they eat the animals as food. During the day, the polyps pull their tentacles back inside their stony houses.

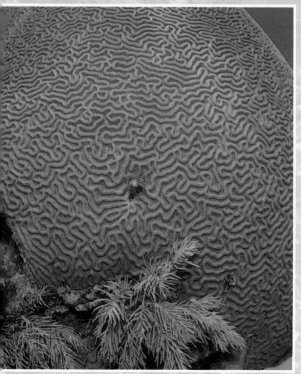

The Coral Reef Neighborhood

Some creatures spend all or most of their lives on the coral reef. Many are strange to look at. Some of the prettiest ones can also be the deadliest to other creatures.

The **sea anemone** is an animal that looks like a flower. Its petals are tentacles that hold a deadly poison. The anemone uses the poison to kill the fish it eats.

The **sponge** is another kind of animal that lives on the coral reef. Sponges may look like small plants. They can also look like tubes, baskets, or sheep's wool.

Sponges provide a home for many other creatures on the reef. Scientists have counted more than 13,000 different creatures—everything from worms and crabs to fish—living in a single sponge!

The **sea urchin** looks like a pin cushion with pins. The spines on its body help protect it from enemies. The spines also help it move about.

The **starfish** is a relative of the sea urchin. It uses tiny cups on its arms to help it move about. If it loses an arm, it just grows a new one.

On the sandy ocean floor between the coral, a **hermit crab** scurries about. These crabs can be as small as a pea or as big as a hand. Hermit crabs climb into old shells that other creatures have left behind. The shells protect them. When a hermit crab grows too big for its shell, it finds a larger one.

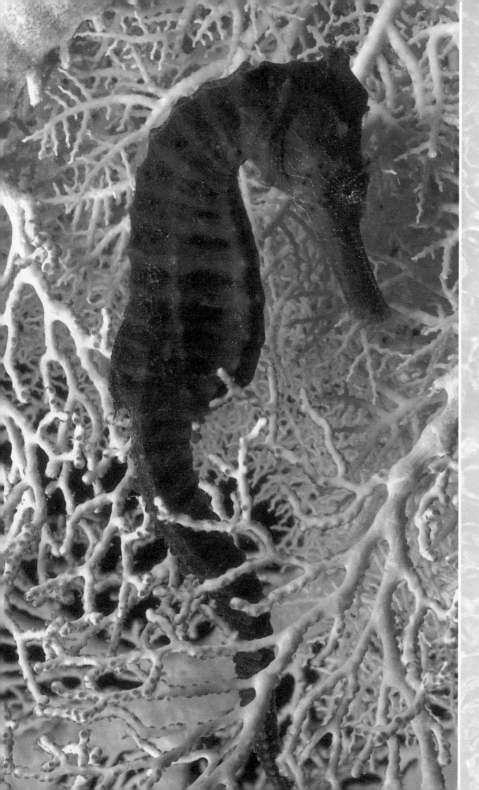

The **sea horse** isn't really a horse at all. It's a kind of fish. Sea horses have no real stomachs, so they must eat all the time to stay alive. A sea horse can eat 2,500 tiny shrimp a day!

Danger on the Reef

The reef is often dangerous for the small fish that live there. That's because they can easily become food for larger fish looking for a meal.

The **butterfly fish** has a special way to fool bigger fish that might eat it. It has a large black spot on both sides of its back. The spots look like eyes. A big fish that is after the butterfly fish can't tell which end is which!

The **trumpet fish** can easily hide from its enemies. It only has to stand on its head in the coral. Its enemies can't even tell that it's there.

The colors and shape of the **spiny lobster** help it to blend in with coral and seaweed. It stays hidden during the day. It comes out only at night to look for food.

To keep from being eaten, the **clownfish** hides among the poisonous tentacles of the sea anemone. The tentacles keep larger fish away, but they don't harm the clownfish. That's because the clownfish first covers itself with a special slime. The slime protects it from the anemone's poison.

To trick its enemies, the **stonefish** uses *camouflage*. That's when the color and other markings on an animal help it hide. The stonefish's camouflage makes it look just like a rock on the ocean floor. But if an enemy does figure out what it is, the stonefish can fight back. It can poison the enemy with one of the spikes on its back.

Some reef fish can change color to hide themselves. The **blue tang** is a bright blue color during the day. But when its enemies come out at night, it changes to gray. That makes it hard to spot in the dark ocean.

An **octopus** can change color in a flash to fool an attacker. It can also change its shape to make it look bigger and tougher. But if an enemy still comes at it, an octopus can shoot out a cloud of black ink. The ink blinds the enemy long enough for the octopus to swim away.

Hunters of the Reef

During the daytime, the **moray eel** hides in the rocks and holes of the reef. When a likely meal swims by, the eel darts out and grabs it. At night, the eel hunts along the bottom of the reef for sea urchins and other creatures. It slithers through the water like a snake does on land.

Like the eel, the **grouper** waits quietly among the coral until a meal swims by. Some groupers get as big as a half a ton in weight! That's about the weight of an adult polar bear. Groupers that big can gulp fish as long as four feet in one bite.

Many types of sharks visit the reef. The **white-tip reef shark** does a lot of hunting there, mostly at night. It eats fish, crabs, lobsters, and octopuses. When it sees a meal swim by, it darts out and snatches it.

The **barracuda** is a tough and scary hunter. It can shoot through the dark water like lightning. With its daggerlike teeth, it can eat a fish in one clean bite. It has even been known to attack people.

How the Coral Reef Neighborhood Works

The reef neighborhood may seem like a cruel place, but the creatures who live there depend on each other for food. This arrangement is called the *food chain,* or food web.

Some of the creatures help each other out in other ways too. Tiny fish, like the **goby** and **wrasse**, help clean the teeth of bigger fish. They pick small bits of food from the larger fish's teeth. The larger fish get their teeth cleaned. The smaller fish get a free meal. This kind of partnership is called *symbiosis.*

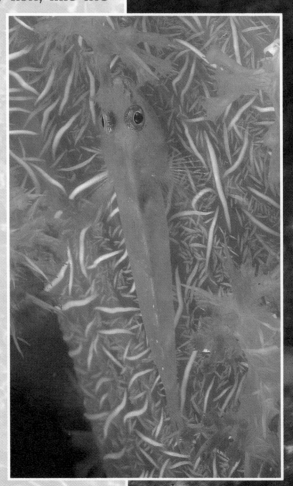

24

People Need the Coral Reef

Sea creatures aren't the only ones who need the reef. People do too. They get fish and other seafood from it. Some reef creatures may even be sources of drugs that fight deadly diseases in people.

Coral reefs also surround many islands, which protect them from harsh waves.

But coral reefs and many of its creatures are disappearing. Scientists aren't sure why, but they think water pollution and oil spills are partly to blame.

Some scientists also believe that air pollution causes the earth and oceans to become warmer. They think that even a small change in the yearly weather conditions, or *climate*, might hurt coral reefs.

Scientists do know that visitors to the reef can be harmful. Divers and ships sometimes break off parts of the coral reef.

They also know that certain creatures — like some starfish — eat the coral from the reef. That can cause the reef a lot of damage.

27

Help For
Coral Reefs

People *are* helping coral reefs. Old ships and oil rigs may seem useless on land. But many have been sunk to help form coral reefs. Once the ships or rigs are on the ocean floor, coral attaches itself to their sides. Together they become part of a whole new reef neighborhood.

28

What You Can Do

You can help the coral reefs too. If you see coral being sold in stores, it's a good idea not to buy it. The coral came from a reef somewhere under the sea.

You can also learn more about coral reefs so that you can tell people how important they are. Many zoos and aquariums have coral reef displays where you can view reef neighborhoods for yourself.

If you want more information about how to help, write to the places below. They'll let you know other ways that you can make a real difference.

National Coalition for Marine Conservation
5105 Paulsen Street, Suite 243
Savannah, Georgia 31405

Friends of the Earth
218 D Street SE
Washington, D. C. 20003

National Audubon Society
950 Third Avenue
New York, New York 10022

National Wildlife Fund
1400 16th Street NW
Washington, D. C. 20037

Glossary

camouflage — the color and other markings on an animal that allow it to hide without being seen.

climate — the general, yearly weather conditions of an area.

equator — an imaginary line that divides the earth into two halves called the Northern and Southern Hemispheres. The equator is the warmest part of the earth.

food chain — the way plants and animals depend on each other for life-giving food and energy.

habitat — the neighborhood, or environment, in which a plant or animal lives.

limestone — a stone, made mostly of a mineral called calcium, that makes up a coral reef.

polyp — a tiny ocean animal, usually no larger than a pea, whose limestone skeletons make up a coral reef.

reef — the limestone ridges and hills built by the coral polyps that are found in warm, shallow ocean waters.

tentacles — the long arms, or feelers, that creatures like octopuses, coral polyps, and sea anemones have.

symbiosis — a partnership between two living things in which both help each other out.

For Further Reading

Berger, Gilda. *The Coral Reef: What Lives There.* New York: Coward, McCann, and Geoghegan, 1977.

Burgess, Robert. *Exploring a Coral Reef.* New York: MacMillan Publishing, 1972.

Cooper, Jason. *The Sea: Coral Reefs.* Vero Beach, Florida, 1992.

Fine, John. *Creatures of the Sea.* New York: Antheneum, 1987.

Johnston, Damian. *Make Your Own Coral Reef.* New York: HarperCollins, 1993.

Lampton, Christopher. *Coral Reefs in Danger.* Connecticut: Millbrook, 1992.

McGovern, Ann. *The Underwater World of the Coral Reef.* New York: Four Winds Press, 1976.

Sargent, William. *Night Reef: Dusk to Dawn on a Coral Reef.* New York: Franklin Watts, 1991.

INDEX